Television

N Chokkan

Television
© *N Chokkan*

First Edition: December 2009
64 Pages
Printed in India.

ISBN 978–81–8493–321–5
Pro–ya–en–57

Prodigy Books
177/103, First Floor, Ambal's Building
Lloyds Road, Royapettah, Chennai 600 014.
Ph: +91-44-4200-9603
Email: support@nhm.in
Website: www.nhm.in

Prodigy Books is an imprint of New Horizon Media Pvt. Ltd.

Contents

The little Genie

Have you heard the *Aladin* story?

Aladin rubbed a small lamp, and out came a genie. It had the power to bring anything that *Aladin* asked for.

Don't you wish for one such genie in your life too? Once you have it, all you need to do is 'ask', and the very next minute the genie will bring it for you, whatever it may be!

In fact, there is one such genie in your own house. Though it can't bring the things you ask for, it can show them to you as if they were real! Look around… are you able to spot that genie?

Yes, it is the Television. Just imagine - how many things this little box brings to us – it is a feast to our eyes: cartoons, movies, games, songs, scenery, general knowledge and much more.

Ten years back, we didn't have so many television channels. There were only a few, and you had to watch whatever they telecast. But today, technology has advanced so much that we have the entire world in our hands. There are hundreds of channels telecasting different kinds of programs - all you need to do is choose what you want and press the remote button!

Still, many people consider the television an "idiot box". Why? Is the television really an idiot box? Or, is it making us dumb?

To find an answer to these questions, you need to understand this wonderful device called television. Only then can you make a decision on how to make best use of this genie in the drawing room.

You watch television everyday. Now, for a change, let us 'read' about television. Join me in this fascinating journey!

Broadcasting Pictures

Before we start, here's a small exercise for you. Just switch off your TV, and think about this: television programmes are recorded in some corner of the world, they are telecast from some other corner, and finally you see them on the television set, with superb clarity and quality. How?

Television is one of the finest technological advancements of the modern world. It is complex for sure, but not very difficult to understand.

Let us explore this with the help of an example: Let's say, you have drawn a nice picture – a cute penguin stands with a flag in its hand, and you have used all your crayons liberally to decorate your art.

Wow! This looks cool. Now you wish to share this wonder creation with someone, your best friend Anu would love to see it. But unfortunately, Anu is in another city. So, how would you share your painting with her?

You can make a photo copy of this art and send it to Anu by post, or by email. But this would take few hours, or even days. You can't wait that long, this has to be shared now, this very instance!

So, you pickup the telephone and dial Anu's number, 'Hey, Guess what I did just now?'

Anu is excited too, 'Tell me, quick'.

'I have drawn a penguin, it looks wonderful'.

'Fantastic! Tell me about it!'

Though you may use all your brains to 'explain' the drawing, there is no assurance that Anu at the other end of the phone would understand it fully.

Worse, listening to your words, she may imagine a totally different picture in her mind. That would be bad, isn't it?

Now let us approach the same problem from a different angle, and try to find a solution. What kind of paper do you use for drawing your paintings — the usual plain white sheet?

For a change, let us use a special sheet with lots of horizontal and vertical lines. Look at the picture below — the lines form a neat grid of small boxes.

If you don't have one such sheet in your house, don't worry, all you need to do is, take a sheet of white paper and draw lines similar to this. Well, how many lines do we need? There are no hard and fast rules here. You can draw as many lines as you want, the more the better.

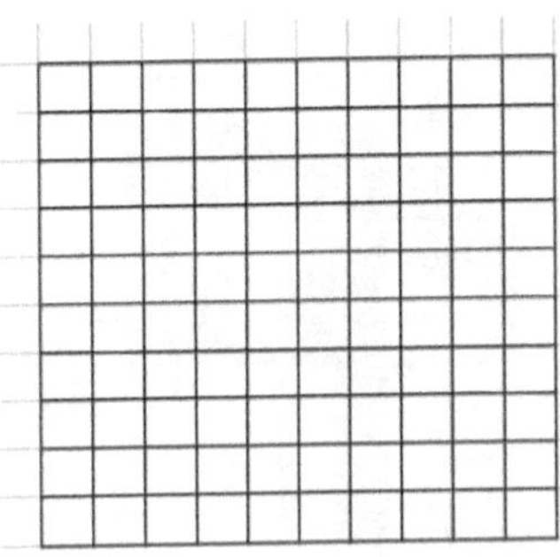

Now, let us start labelling them. Horizontal lines can be labelled as A, B, C, D… and so on, and vertical lines as 1, 2, 3, 4, and so on. Look at the picture below and make sure your drawing looks exactly like this:

Now, we shall draw our special picture in this special sheet. It is very easy — all we need to do is start shading some of these boxes in our special sheet, and form a neat drawing. Look at the shaded picture — it will give you an idea of how it is to be done.

This picture looks very odd, right? That's because we have only 100 small boxes in this picture. But when you increase this number to 1000 or more, you can draw paintings that are much more beautiful.

Now that the drawing is ready, how are you going to send it to Anu? Very Simple! Call Anu over the phone and explain to her about your 'special' sheet of paper. Ask her to prepare a similar sheet.

Now, watch your sheet carefully, and note down all the boxes that you have shaded black - 3B, 4B, 5B, 6B, 7B, 3C, 4C, 6C, and so on. Now read out these numbers to Anu and ask her to blacken the same boxes in her sheet with a pencil. Within a few minutes, Anu will also have a picture that looks exactly like yours — quite simple and amazing, isn't it?

The same principle is used in television technology too. In contrast to the picture drawn by hand, advanced machines create the pictures. These pictures are then transmitted on air that are received by our television set and displayed on the screen. But wait, there's something wrong here! A picture doesn't move. But the images we see on the television move. How is this possible?

You won't believe this — the fact is that the images displayed on the television are purely static. They don't move at all. Instead, they display a series of pictures very fast, so that we feel a sense of 'movement'. It's a trick played by our eyes and the brain.

Before we discuss this further, we need to understand how our brain works!

Moving Pictures

Do you have a lens at home? Pick up a newspaper or magazine or your favourite book. Select any colour image printed on it, and observe it carefully using your lens. What do you see? A series of dots!

A printed picture comprises of a number of dots, which are held closely together. But when we actually see them, they don't look like dots. We can clearly see Tom & Jerry, or Sachin Tendulkar, or Shah Rukh Khan, or scenery. How? It is the brain that makes us see them as complete pictures.

Now let us do another small experiment.

Take a small, thick sheet of paper. Make small holes on two of its sides. Draw a picture of a ball - a cricket ball, football, tennis ball or basket ball. Turn the sheet over, and on the other side, draw a square. Make sure its size is bigger than the ball on the other side.

Take a long thread and cut it into two halves. Tie them to the two holes of your sheet. Hold the two ends of the thread in your hands, and rotate the sheet in between, very fast. What do you see? The ball is inside the box! How?

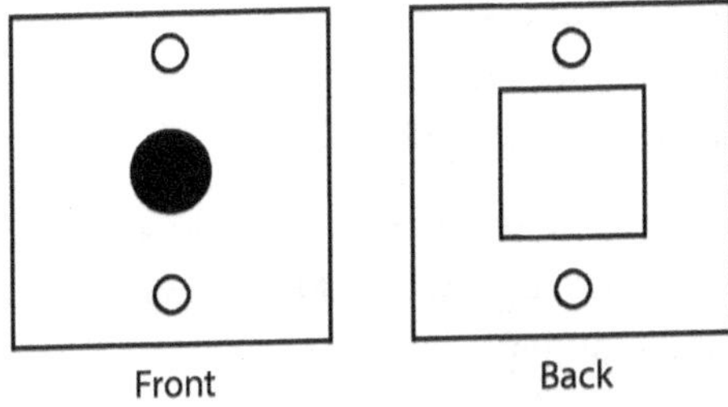

We drew the ball and box separately, on two different sides of the sheet. Still, it looks as if the ball has jumped into the box on the other side.

This is another trick played by our brain. Even though these two images are separate, our brain makes us believe that it is a single image because we see them next to each other repeatedly.

Let us try to apply the same principle to television technology. You are watching news on the television in which our Prime Minister appears and waves his hands. Though it looks like a moving image, in reality, it is nothing but a series of pictures, seen next to each other.

Here too, our brain makes us believe that the Prime Minister is actually 'moving'.

Now, let us just take six images:

1. The Prime Minister appears on the screen.
2. His hand moves up.
3. Hand goes above his shoulder.
4. Hand goes above his head.
5. Hand moves left.
6. Hand moves right.

When we see these six images in rapid succession, what we have is the moving image of the Prime Minister lifting his hand and waving!

This small trick played by the brain forms the basis for television technology. Instead of six images, they show six hundred, six thousand or six million images continuously, and we can see various actions performed by characters on screen.

To summarize, Television is nothing but a box, which shows lots and lots of images rapidly, and creates an illusion that those images are actually moving.

But, how does the television show these pictures?

Behind the Screen

Do you watch cricket Live on the television?

If you observe carefully, almost every cricket ground has a giant board, in which they display the score, how many runs each batsman has made, how many wickets have fallen, and many other interesting statistics.

Sometimes, when a batsman scores a half century or century, the same scoreboard displays beautiful animation art and congratulates him. Modern scoreboards go one level up and display video on these screens. Spectators can therefore watch replays on the scoreboards!

When we look at these screens from a distance, they seem like magical devices. But if we go closer to it and observe, we will be disappointed. These electronic scoreboards are nothing but a series of small bulbs held closely together. When a few bulbs glow in unison, it displays the score or animation.

Now, can you relate this to what we learnt in the previous chapter? When there are a series of dots placed next to each other, our brain understands that it is a picture or a drawing. The same technology is used in these scoreboards also.

The television also has a similar concept. Instead of bulbs, the television has tiny dot-like phosphors which may glow in a certain pattern to complete the picture we see on the screen.

Before we get there, let us get introduced to an important part of television. It's called CRT – the Cathode Ray Tube. You would have studied about Cathodes and Anodes in your Chemistry lessons – they act against each other, as positive and negative nodes.

In electronics, anodes are called positive terminals and cathodes are negative terminals. They have been named so because of their properties—cathodes emit electrons, which are negatively charged and anodes being positive, absorb these electrons and control them.

Now, coming back to CRT, each letter in it is of great significance. Hence we need to understand it clearly before we learn how a television works. For a change, let us start from the last letter – T.

'T' stands for a long cylindrical glass tube. We can easily see this tube in our television set. Just look at the screen, it is one end of a long CR Tube!

The specialty of this tube is that it's filled with nothing!

Nothing? Yes, we call it void, absolute nothing-ness. But why should we make this tube void?

The answer lies in the next character– R.

'R' stands for ray, an electron ray. When we heat the cathode, which is a negative terminal, it emits electrons. The collection of electrons is called a "Ray".

But the electrons that are emitted from a cathode won't become a ray automatically. They will run in whichever direction they want — exactly like how children run around, when the school gates are opened! So, what the teachers do? They control the children and make them form a line, and direct them to the bus.

We need to do something similar here, to control these naughty electrons into proper Rays. Otherwise, the electrons will run to every corner of the CRT and will become useless.

This is where the anodes come into the picture, 'Excuse me, may I come in?'

But, this is a Cathode Ray Tube, why do we need anodes here?

Just like a school that needs teachers, a CRT also requires the services of anodes, mainly to control the electrons emitted by the cathode.

Have you heard the story of Pied Piper of Hamelin? There was a beautiful village. But all the houses in the village were infested with rats, lots and lots of them! To get rid of these nasty creatures, they went to the Piper for help: 'Please help us! We will pay you whatever you want.'

Next day, the Piper came to the village, played his magical music instrument and all the rats followed him in a neat straight line. The rats that ran around the house were disciplined by the Piper. They stopped being naughty and started walking in unison, in a direction pointed out by the Piper.

No wonder it's a fairy tale. But in real life too, there are some 'Pied Piper moments' when certain things get attracted to few other things. Take magnets for example. Every magnet has a North pole and a South pole. The North pole of one magnet attracts the South pole of another, and vice versa.

Similarly, two North poles will repel each other. The same is true for two South poles. Now, let us play a game. Take two small magnets of same size. Mark their North and South poles clearly.

Now, keep one magnet on a table, and another in your hand. Let us call them T and H accordingly. Move the North pole of magnet H slowly towards the South pole of magnet T. What happens? Magnet T moves a little, and tries to touch the magnet H in your hand. If you move magnet H any closer, magnet T may even jump and stick to the other magnet. This is because North and South poles attract each other. Slowly move magnet H away from the table. Observe what magnet T does. It starts moving further and further. If you do it slowly and with care, you can make magnet T move in any direction you want to.

So we may conclude that the North-South attraction of a magnet can be used to control its movement and direction.

The same concept is used inside the CRT. Instead of North-South, we have Plus-Minus here. Because the attraction between these polarities is equally strong, we can use anodes to control the movement of cathodes in any direction — especially towards the television screen.

That's why we have anodes inside a Cathode Ray Tube. These anodes are called "Focusing Anodes". There is another type of anode, which are not used for focusing, but for increasing the speed of Electron Ray movement. They are called "Accelerating Anodes".

Observe the picture below carefully — the electrons that are emitted from the cathode are controlled, accelerated, and focused by anodes, and finally hit the screen at the other end of the CRT.

The specialty of this screen is that it's coated with phosphor. When electrons hit phosphor, it glows brightly. This natural

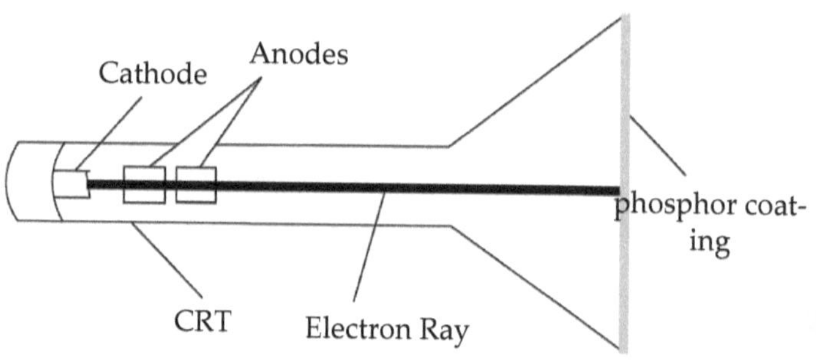

property of phosphor is used in television technology. The "picture" we watch on the television is nothing but a glow of phosphor on the screen. This takes different shapes at different timings and makes us believe as if the pictures are moving.

But wait, when you look at this picture, it looks as if all the electrons hit the same spot on the middle of the screen. Then how does it become a picture which occupies the entire screen?

There is a simple technology behind this too — it is called Magnetic Field!

Scanning 60 times per second

I have a big magnet, which I have placed in the centre of this room. My friend is standing in a corner of the same room. He has a small nail in his hand.

According to science, magnets attract iron. But this magnet doesn't seem to be attracting my friend's nail. Why? Simply because he is standing far away from the magnet. If he comes closer and moves the nail towards the magnet, it will grab the piece of iron immediately.

When the nail was away from magnet, it was not able to attract it. But when it was brought closer, the attraction worked like magic. This limit is called a Magnetic Field.

Almost all things have some magnetism or the other — even the earth we live. Some of these are strong magnets, others are weak.

There is a small trick to create a strong magnetic field in a metal object — simply pass electricity over it. The magnetic field thus created is aptly called Electro Magnetic Field. But what does this do to television?

Just recall what we learnt about CRT. Cathodes emit electrons, which are controlled by anodes, forming a straight ray. This ray hits the screen in the centre. But if the ray stays in the centre, it cannot be put to use. We need to pull it to every corner of the screen so that the television can show us pictures and moving images. This is where the Electro Magnetic Field comes to our help!

Metal objects are fixed on all the sides of a CRT, where two strong Electro Magnetic Fields are created — one to move electrons up and down and another to move them left and right.

To summarise, we may conclude on the following:
- Cathodes emit electrons.
- They are focused and accelerated by anodes.
- Electron ray hits the phosphor screen.
- Two Electro Magnetic Fields move it all over the screen, forming pictures.

People call television a "small screen" but it is a very big screen! If you don't believe me, switch off your television. Go near the screen and observe carefully, you can see several tiny circles or dots.

Each one of these circles is coated with phosphor. When electrons hit them from the other side of the CRT, they glow brightly. But it is not enough if one or two phosphor dots glow at a time. Like a paint brush which helps draw a picture, the electron ray should move around all these phosphor dots on the screen, up and down, left and right. This process is called Scanning.

The method in which an electron ray scans a phosphor screen is very interesting. Many television sets use different techniques for this, but the basic concept is same.

To understand this better, just observe the postman in your area. How does he ensure the prompt delivery of letters at every house? First, he starts with the house in the corner. Then he moves to the second, no letters there. So he goes to the next (third) house and delivers some letters, moves on to the next, and so on, till the whole street is scanned and completed.After that? He has to move to another street (or the other side of the same street) and start all over again. If he does it in every street allotted to him, then all the letters will be delivered promptly.

The electron ray inside a CRT does almost the same type of scanning:

1. It starts with the top left corner phosphor dot.

2. It finishes the entire first row — left to right. It may hit few dots and skip some others.

3. The dots hit by the electron rays will glow brightly or dimly, depending on the strength of the ray. Other dots will remain in the dark.

4. After scanning the first row, it jumps from the right side to the left side. (Look at the picture).

5. Now, it starts scanning the second row.

6. It repeats the same, until all rows are completely scanned.

7. Once again, it jumps to the first row – top left corner (step 1 above) and continues scanning.

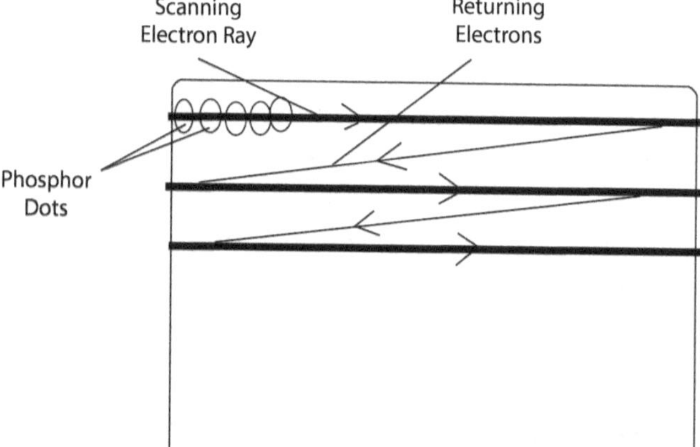

Ah, that's a lot—Imagine cathode rays doing it 60 times a second! Yes! A second is a small fraction of time, but electrons are super fast, they finish all the scanning 60 times, before we can say 'wow'.

Because of this fast scanning, the images on the television keep changing continuously. And our brain makes us believe that the images are actually moving!

The CRT technology we have seen till now is present in almost every television and is called by the name, Picture Tube.

Next, it is time for some colourful fun!

The Magic of Colours

How many colours you know of? How many do you think exist in this world—seven, ten, fifteen or a thousand? In reality, there are only three basic colours. If we mix these three in different combinations, we can form any number of new colours.

The three basic colors are RGB: Red, Green, Blue.

These are the only "real" colours in this world. All other colours are derived from these three. For example:

- o Mix Red, Green and Blue in equal proportions, and you get <u>White.</u>
- o Mix Red and Green equally, you get <u>Yellow.</u>
- o Mix Red and Blue equally, you get <u>Magenta.</u>
- o Mix Red, Green and Blue in a ratio of 195:176:145, you get <u>Khaki.</u>

This is just a small sample. In a similar way, we can make millions of such combinations and form new colours. All are derivatives of the basic (RGB) colours.

So, if you want to use hundreds of colours in your painting, you don't have to buy all of them. Just buy Red, Green and Blue, mix them in different ratios and make the other colours that you may need!

The television also does the same. It uses the three basic colours and mixes them to produce other colours as and when necessary.

Look at the picture below. It's the same CRT Tube. But now we have three cathode rays instead of one. Let us call them R–G–B rays.

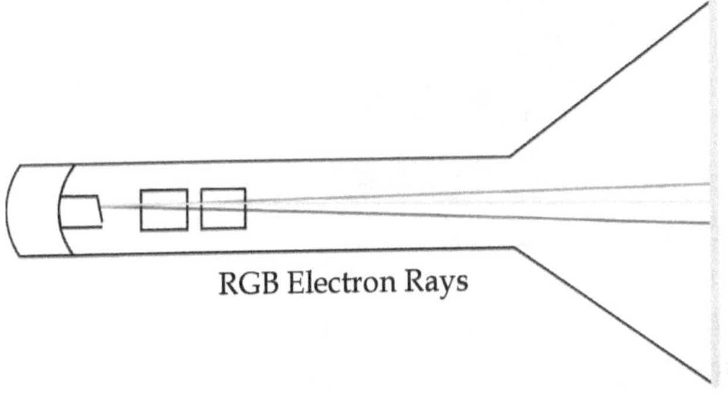

RGB Electron Rays

When electron rays hit the phosphor coating, they glow. But to make them glow in different colours, it is not enough if you have a single phosphor coating; you need at least three – Red, Green and Blue. Using these three basic colour coatings in different combinations, you can create all other required colours.

The following picture shows how these three coatings appear on your television. They may be created as small dots, or bands. The shape really doesn't matter, all we need is, electrons hitting the three coatings with different ratios and creating the colours on the screen.

CRT Screen with phosphor coatings in three colours

For example, if a dot in the television has to display blue colour, only one of the three cathode rays falls there, that too on the blue coating, creating a blue glow.

On the next dot, we need to show yellow. So, when two cathode rays hit both Red and Green coatings, the mixture creates a yellow glow.

If a third dot has to show white colour, all three cathode rays hit their respective coatings, and a white glow is produced.

Now, if the fourth dot has to show black, all three cathode rays will skip the dot or its RGB coatings, making it a perfect black.

In modern televisions, there are many new technologies which produce millions of colours and sharp pictures. But the basic concept behind CRT remains almost the same. In the last half century, CRT is one of the most widely used technologies in a variety of devices.

We have now understood how CRT produces beautiful pictures and moving images. But where do these pictures come from?

Recording and Broadcasting

I am a big lover of Rock music shows and live concerts. Are you?

The only problem with these great events is that there are just too many people around and not everyone can look at the stage or the musicians clearly.

There is a simple solution for this—put up giant video screens all around. Now people in any corner can watch them, listen to the music and enjoy the experience thoroughly.

This small example helps us understand how television programmes are recorded and telecast. Let us start with a simple question: *How are these rock music events recorded?*

That's very easy. You can see one or more videographers running around with cameras. They capture every musician, singer and others on the stage; sometimes they record the fans and their excitement too. The term "recording" means capturing the events on a tape, or a digital storage device, which is generally present within the camera.

Almost all the programmes we watch on television are recorded using a similar camera. So let us explore how this magic device works.

In fact, a camera is not new to us. It's just the opposite of what we have discussed till now! Let us brush up a little - what happens inside a television? Electricity produces electron rays and it creates moving images on our screen.

A camera does just the reverse—it "watches" moving images, and converts them into electrical signals. These changes in the signals are recorded permanently for future use. For this, a camera has two important parts: Lens and Recorder.

All cameras have one or more lenses. By moving them front or back, we can record any event happening around us. But a camera can see and record only if there is light. It may be natural, or created artificially using a focus lamp.

Either way, things around us reflect light, some are bright and others are dull. This difference is carefully captured by the camera, gets converted to electric signals, and is recorded in a tape or a memory chip.

Modern cameras have a small screen attached to them. This can be used to replay the recorded video immediately, and reshoot if necessary.

But how does the camera send the pictures to a video screen far away? Actually, cameras don't send any images anywhere, their job is just to record the events, and convert them to electric signals before storing them.

Once this is done, the electric signals are sent to one or more places by few other devices. This process is called "telecasting". In a rock concert, the recorded video may be telecast using wires. These wires carry the electric signals to the giant screens, which simply convert them to moving images again.

But we can't rely on wires for every telecast. For example, when a cricket match happens, it is not possible to connect the cameras in the playground to every television set in the world.

To solve this problem, our scientists have invented several wonderful solutions like transmission. If your favourite singer is in Mumbai, singing a fantastic song, and you are in Chennai, is it possible for you to enjoy the song? Let us explore this technology in detail.

First, there is a camera in Mumbai, in front of your favourite artist. It captures his every movement, which gets recorded in a tape or a computer.

And what about the sound? Is it recorded too?

Sure. Without sound, how can you enjoy your song?

Watch carefully. There is a mike (microphone) in your singer's hand, or is fixed onto his dress. This tiny device records all the sounds around it, exactly like how a camera records moving images.

Mikes are equipped to capture even a tiny sound nearby. They later convert these sounds into electric signals, which are recorded for storage and replay.

So, we now have two signals:

- Image signals coming from the camera
- Sound signals coming from the microphone

But we are not happy with just the sound, or the video. Fun starts only when we combine these two. Television studios are special rooms where such recording and mixing can be done. Once this is completed, the signals are ready for telecast.

For this purpose, television studios have some special devices called transmitters. You might have seen television transmitters around you. They are huge cone-shaped towers rising towards the sky. On the top, there will be a small antenna. There are two types of antennas:

- Transmitting Antennas
  Receiving Antennas

As the name suggests, Transmitting antennas are used to send video and audio signals. Receiving antennas accept them and play the images and sound.

A transmitting antenna is equipped to convert video and audio recordings into Electromagnetic waves, which can be sent on air. Transmitters can send many such programmes simultaneously. For example, there are channels for news, movies, music, sports, cartoons and so on. These may be telecast from the same transmitter or many.

What happens next? How does the signal transmitted from Mumbai or Delhi reach the television set in our home? To understand this, let us observe another simple real life scenario — speaking.

When two people talk to each other, what happens between them? How do the sound waves coming from one person's mouth reach the other person's ear?

Quite simple. They travel in the air between them!

A television transmitter also does the same. Whether it is a song, a dance, a sports event, or a cartoon, it converts everything to Electromagnetic waves and spreads them in the air.

But air is everywhere. How can we bring these waves to our house, through our television set? This is where the receiving antennas are useful. Their job is to absorb the Electromagnetic waves in air, and send them to our television set.

But I am still concerned about one thing — about the waves in the air. Won't it be too dangerous to leave them there? Will they be able to travel long distances?

Oh sure! Television programmes travel across cities, states and countries. The whole world can watch the programmes transmitted from any corner. For this purpose, transmitters use satellite technology.

Certain man made satellites are put into the earth's orbit. We can't see them, but they are always there. Some of them take pictures, some do research in space, some are used as GPS satellites to locate things, and so on. Let us focus on the satellites which are used for telecasting video and audio programmes. They are called communication satellites. These receive signals sent by transmitters and transmit them to the whole world. By doing so, they simply increase the reach of the television programmes.

To understand how and why satellites help in television technology, let us perform another small experiment. There is a hall, where 100 people are gathered. You need to make a speech that will be audible to all of them. Where will you stand and deliver the speech?

If you stand in the middle of the room and speak, some of the people in the nearest circle can easily see you and hear you. But what about others? There is no assurance that everybody can listen and understand your speech.

Instead, you climb to a stage on one side of the hall. Now, everybody can see you clearly. What is the difference between the two methods described here? The height!

When you are on a raised platform, your words spread automatically from the elevated position, and more people will be able to absorb what you are saying.

Apply the same principle for satellites: they are in a much higher position than regular transmitters. So they can spread the television programmes to many more locations easily.

If we use more than one satellite for communication, television programmes can easily reach the antennas of homes all over the globe.

But my television set does not come with an antenna, and I can still watch the programmes. How is that?

Direct to Home

Till a few years back, whenever someone bought a television, they got a metallic antenna with it. They would go to the roof top, fix the antenna, and turn it in a specific direction before they can start watching the programmes. What happened to those antennas now? These days no house seems to be having antennas on top. But still, they are able to enjoy the television programmes. How?

The simple reason is, the antenna receiver technology we discussed earlier, has become very old and almost outdated now. There are much more sophisticated and clear technologies in the market today. For example, let us take something we are familiar with – Cable TV. In case of regular TV, the programme signals are telecast on air, as electromagnetic waves. They are captured by the receiver antenna in our house, as explained already.

But today's cable TV carries all the signals required directly into your house. So you don't need any antenna on the roof to receive the signals. The signals received through cables directly reach your television set. The signals are instantly converted into pictures, which we can start watching immediately.

The cable TV has its own limitations — it can only have a limited network that can spread to certain areas. You cannot connect to a far off place away from your city through cables — it will be very expensive.

Then why should we opt for cable TV at all? Why not adopt the television's old model?

Earlier, all television signals were telecast only on air and people had to fix an antenna for watching the programmes. But people living in the hilly areas couldn't get television signals properly. They either received blank screens, or worse — unclear, jumping pictures — which spoilt the whole experience. As people started complaining, scientists started thinking of an alternative.

As a result, cable TV was introduced in 1948. It allows people in a certain region to watch television programmes without the need for an antenna.

In a cable TV setup, there will be a cable TV operator or service provider who is responsible for getting the signals from various television stations and other content providers. For this, they may either use a big dish-shaped antenna or other advanced technologies.

They transmit the signals received through cables to the houses in and around their area. For this, they charge a monthly subscription fee. The concept is very simple — instead of every house keeping a small antenna, a single operator gets the signals and shares them with others!

As an extension to the cable TV system, there is a new technology that is now catching up — the satellite television. An important benefit of satellite television is that it offers superb picture clarity, combined with a wide range of channels. Depending on this you can choose your own channels out of the hundreds or even thousands available.

Since the option to pick the channels is with the subscriber, somebody interested in sports may ignore movie channels, or vice versa. And everyone pays only for what the ones chosen, and it is quite economical.

Additionally, satellite televisions can also provide movies on demand — you can download and watch the latest movies from the comfort of your home, and at a time convenient to you. If you want to opt for satellite television, you may have to fix a small dish antenna at home. This would be a smaller version of what the cable TV operators have. Once this dish is fixed on your roof or balcony, and the television is tuned, all programmes will reach your home directly. That's why this technology is also called DTH – Direct To Home!

Other than these programmes, we also watch at home the CD/DVD. When you play those movies or other videos, you actually telecast a programme, which only you alone can watch. All these signals reach our home through different technologies and are converted in such a way that they get displayed on our television screen properly.

For this, some special devices called tuners are used which split the picture, sound, and other information separately, and send them to the television set in an appropriate manner. This sound/picture information is used by the cathode ray tube in your television. Finally, we are able to enjoy our favourite programme.

One important thing to be remembered is that even though these things sound very complex, they are happening all around you every minute, every second. Various television channels and companies across the globe produce different kinds of programmes on a regular basis and telecast them regularly. Our televisions act as the windows to the world, literally. All you need is a small remote control!

Remote control? We haven't discussed about this wonder device yet – how this little electronic instrument helps us enhance our TV watching experience? Let us explore this in detail!

Remote Control

In the earlier days, televisions had no remote control!

Oops! It must have been very difficult—every time you want to change the channel, you need to get up, go near the television, touch a small switch or knob there and turn it. Same for increasing and decreasing volume, adjusting the brightness or even switching it on/off!

Thank god, we now have remote controls. We can sit in one corner of the house, and with the push of a button, we can do anything we want to with regard to the television. As the name suggests, remote controls can order and control a television set. It's the ultimate form of authority.

But remember, remote control is NOT part of your television. Any TV will work perfectly well even without a remote control. In reality, many people don't even want to think about it. For them, remote control is a sign of supreme energy, if someone grabs it from their hands, they feel powerless.

So, what is inside a remote control? Just like your television, the remote control is also an electronic device. But compared to the television, it is much simpler.

Basically, a remote control contains an electronic circuit. To be more specific, it is an incomplete electronic circuit. Why is it incomplete? What do we need to make it complete?

Simply press any button on your remote, the circuit closes and a light glows on one end of the remote control device. Light? That's surprising! I have never seen a light in any remote control!

True. Because, the light that glows on a remote control can't be seen with the naked eye. But it is always there. You must have studied about rainbows in school? What are the seven colours you see in a rainbow?

VIBGYOR – Violet, Indigo, Blue, Green, Yellow, Orange and Red. These seven colours can be seen with the naked eye. But there are some colours that have a wavelength beyond that of red, which is not visible to us. They are called infrared rays.

Every remote control has a small bulb at one end, which can emit infrared rays. This bulb is called LED – Light

Emitting Diode. This LED is linked to every button in our remote control. So, when you press a button, the circuit gets closed and signal goes to the LED. According to the button pressed, the LED emits a different combination of infrared rays.

For example, if you want to change to channel number 7, you press the button 7. If you want to increase the volume, you press the button marked as Volume+.

In both these cases, your action was same—pressing a button. But depending on which button you pressed, the LED's infrared output will be different, creating a totally different set of infrared rays.

The infrared rays are not visible to us. But there is a special device in your television which can read this and understand it too. It is called the sensor. If you want to test this, point your remote in a direction other than the television, and press a button. What happens?

Nothing! You keep pressing many buttons, but there is no reaction on the television. This is because the sensor in your television is not able to read the infrared rays even though the LEDs emit them. Because you are pointing the LED bulb in a different direction, the rays can't reach the sensor at all.

Once the sensor catches the infrared signals properly, it understands what is to be done. Take the same example where the channel has to change to 7, or the volume has to be increased. For this, a remote control needs power. Turn your television remote over; there are one or more batteries fixed there, which provide the necessary power for its operations.

These days, almost every device in our home has a remote control—television, music player, CD/DVD player, air conditioner, or even to close/open doors, window curtains and so on. To avoid having multiple remote controls for so many appliances, there is a technology where many remote controls can be programmed into a single device. Then you don't have to juggle with numerous remote controls and can operate all of them with a single hand-held device.

Australian scientists have gone one level ahead of these traditional remote controls. Their innovation uses our hand gestures for controlling the television. For this, a small camera is fixed on top of the television. This camera watches us, and depending on our hand gestures, it changes the television behaviour.

Consider this example: you are watching a television programme. It is boring, and you want to change the channel. Now, instead of searching for a remote, simply move your hands and make a 'Thumbs up' gesture. The camera on top of the television watches this signal, and immediately moves to the next channel. That's all!

What if I want to return to the old channel again? Very simple. Just show a 'Thumbs down' signal!

Similarly, there are hand gestures for every possible television control and you can do without any remote control device in your hand. Amazing, isn't it?

Television technology has become more advanced now and has come a long way since it all began. It is a fascinating story indeed!

The Invention

Do you know who invented the telephone? That's an easy question to answer — Alexander Graham bell! Similarly, if I ask you about inventor of airplane, electricity or gravity you will give the answers in a flash. The answers to these are available from many general knowledge books and encyclopedias.

But tell me, who invented the television? Difficult, isn't it? Surprisingly, there is no single answer to this question. Television is not a product, but a dream! Many people imagined a device like this and thought of creating it. Bits and pieces of ideas slowly came together to create this wonder device sitting in our drawing room.

In fact, much before the television was invented, many people had visualised this dream. Many people have even documented this vision, even though they were not technically qualified to create an actual device.

For example, the Mahabharatha has an interesting story. King Dhridharashtra wanted to witness the war between the Pandavas and Kauravas, live! He couldn't go to the battlefield as he was blind and old.

So, the king summoned his trusted aide, Vidhura who watched the battlefield from the palace and gave the king a live commentary of the happenings.

Stories apart, when did the dream of television become a reality? Who was the achiever? Frankly, we can't name a single inventor for the television. There were many brains behind this and the one of the first models was called a mechanical TV.

In 1894, a German scientist called Paul Nipkow introduced this mechanical television. His invention had two plates, with lots of holes in them – like what you see in this picture.

Nipkow placed one of these plates close to the scene that was to be captured and recorded. The other plate was kept far away, where it was

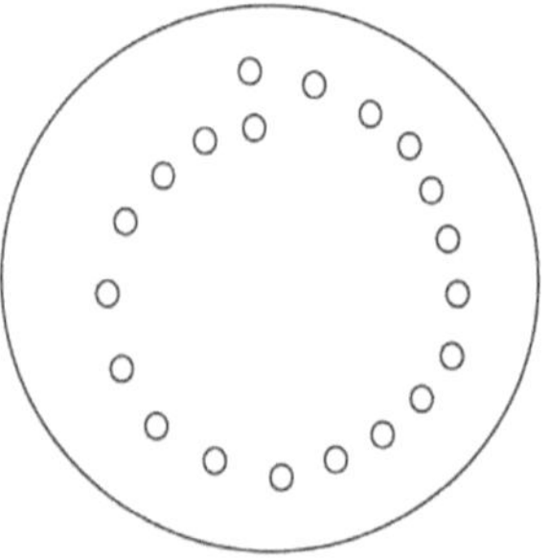

supposed to be played back – something like the modern camera (transmitter) and the television (receiver). Let us assume that we want to record the image of a small doll. We keep one plate near it and rotate it slowly.

When the plate rotates, the light from the doll passes through the holes in the plate, to the other side. This controls the amount of electricity passing through a special apparatus.

For example, if the light is bright, the apparatus will allow ample electricity to pass through it. If the light is dull or dim, then only less electricity passes through. This electricity is sent to a bulb, which will glow accordingly - bright or dim - depending on how much electricity it receives.

Nipkow kept the second plate next to this bulb and rotated it in the same speed as the first plate. Wow! It was like

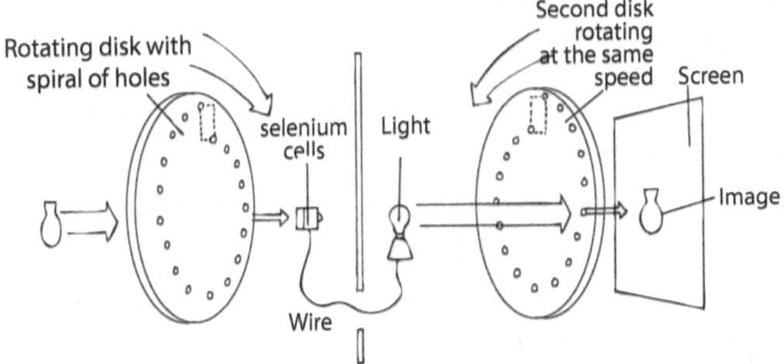

magic! The doll's image, which was recorded earlier in the first plate, showed up next to the second plate. Look at the picture for more clarity on how this early generation television worked.

This looks very simple. But the television created by Nipkow was not that great; it showed pictures of average clarity, and had mixed results. But still, in those days, it was a considerable achievement. Many scientists picked the threads from where Nipkow left and started creating better television models.

It didn't happen fast. Between Nipkow's first model of television, and a reliable, decent invention, it took almost 40 years. There were many scientists who worked on television technology during this period. But two of them deserve a special mention: John Logie Baird and Charles Francis Jenkins.

These two scientists were from different countries, and worked independent of each other, which finally led to a better television.

In 1926, John Logie Baird successfully perfected the Nipkow television technology with so many enhancements. That's why he is termed as the father of modern television science. Baird didn't stop with a simple television device. He wanted to create a television studio, produce programmes, send them across the globe, and so on.

But for such big dreams, Baird's invention was not very good. It was well ahead of its time, but the picture quality was below average and nobody was interested in a full-time television channel with such images.

At the same time, Charles Francis Jenkins also came up with his mechanical television. It was a result of many years of hard work, and the picture quality in Jenkins' television was quite decent. Jenkins named his invention as Radiovision. Then he started telecasting programmes from America's Virginia district to Washington. The American public liked this new model very much. They all wanted to have it in their homes.

But in those days, there were no television studios or telecast centers in America. If people start buying television sets, where are the programmes for them to see? Jenkins saw it as a great opportunity. He decided to start his own television channel. In 1928, the Jenkins Television Corporation was started. Through this company, Jenkins started producing television sets, and the programmes. Of course, we can't compare the programmes of yesteryear with those of today. People had to manage with unreliable picture quality, audio problems and many other issues. But the American public loved them anyway.

Other companies smelled money in this and jumped-in, started their own television companies and channels, which reached even the tiniest of villages. But somebody had to do something about the picture quality and other problems. Otherwise people would get bored and reject the whole concept of television.

Once again, scientists got down to work. The mechanical television gave way for its electronic cousin!

The Future

Almost every modern device we use today, started as a mechanical invention, and later adopted electronics. Television is no exception. When mechanical televisions couldn't hold the public's interest, many people started thinking in the direction of electronics and even succeeded in inventing something similar to today's cathode ray tubes.

These electronic devices had their own problems. One by one, countless scientists worked diligently and removed these bottlenecks to produce a decent electronic television. But there was another major problem — to use an electronic television, you also needed an electronic camera!

There were many scientists who worked on this technology and two of them succeeded in making the electronic camera: Vladimir K Zworykin and Philo T Farnsworth.

Vladimir K Zworykin created a device called the iconoscope. Soon, it became very successful and many individuals and companies started using it in their television cameras. Philo T Farnsworth also produced an almost similar product with superb results. His camera recorded scenes and moving images with wonderful clarity.

After that, nobody had any doubt about the electronic television. Almost every company started adopting this new-age technology. In 1936, Britain's BBC started its telecast and the year became a significant one in the history of television. Compared to the mechanical TV, electronic televisions produced high quality pictures. But they had no colour; all pictures were in black and white only.

Today's generation wouldn't have seen a Black and White television. But at one point of time, it was the only television available. Colours were unheard of. As usual, television manufacturers were looking for a way of selling more TV sets. So they invented a new model of colour television.

Colour televisions became popular only in the mid-1940s. Much earlier, in the early 20th century, many scientists were working on bringing colourful images to television screens. But they were not very successful.

Between 1946 and 1950, two companies made a significant impact to this research — Columbia Broadcasting System

(CBS) and Radio Corporation of America (RCA).

CBS created a cheap colour television but their telecast technology was very specific — it would work only in their special televisions. It was not a great hit with the public because they had to buy new specialised television sets of CBS make to watch their programmes.

This is where RCA scored — they used the existing television technology effectively, to create colour images. Even though their televisions were priced on the higher side, Americans accepted them readily.

From then on, many companies started introducing colour televisions, and the prices also declined gradually. These days, you get a much superior colour television at a fraction of its price many years ago.

Technology is now growing at a rapid pace. Every day a new television model gets introduced into the market with upgraded features, and the public simply seem to love it!

Before we talk more about it, a quick question for you — where do you keep your television set?

Most of the people keep their television in the drawing room in a corner, on the top of a table or have a specially designed cabinet exclusively made for it. Some houses have two television sets — one in the drawing room and another in the bedroom. A few lucky children may even have their own trendy television set in their room.

While building a house, most of them plan a special place for the television. The furniture and décor are generally based on the location of television. Latest technology has brought trendy flat screen television sets into the market. So, most modern homes have no specific area demarcated for the television. You can hang it on the wall, just like a picture or calendar.

Though they may look smaller, they are technologically sound and give clear picture, wonderful colours and exceptional sound—making television watching an enjoyable experience.

One such modern television is called PDP—Plasma Display Panel! PDP televisions have two layers made of glass. Between these layers, gas cells with free flowing, electrically charged ions are filled. These absorb electricity and glow in accordance with the signals the television receives, creating crystal clear images.

When compared to normal television, plasma TVs are extra bright and the picture is sharper. True or not, advertisements claim that once you have watched a plasma TV, you would never settle for anything less.

Recently, another kind of TV is gaining popularity—the LCD TV. A Liquid Crystal Display (LCD) TV uses the same technology as that of portable laptop computers. Compared to other screens, an LCD screen consumes less electricity and computers are adopting this technology to save power. Now television screens are also adopting this technology and give picture quality on par with a plasma television.

Another innovation is the Multimedia Television PC. These televisions act like personal computers—they not only display programmes, but can also record them. This helps you to pause and play television programmes, as and when you like, similar to the replay of a recorded movie.

Imagine you are watching a live cricket match and somebody is there at the door. You don't want to miss the cricket, and at the same time can't ignore the visitor too. This is where recordable multimedia PC televisions are of great help. You can watch a music concert on one channel and also record your mother's favourite cookery programme from another.

As an extension to multimedia PC television, we now have something called Internet TV! As the name suggests, internet television programmes are telecast on various websites. Be it news, sports, literary discussions or business shows, the programmes are webcast from a centralised server and any computer can receive these and play them back too, live or recorded. Even though the name is Internet television, you really don't need a television set to watch it. All you need is a computer and high speed internet connectivity!

Friend or Foe

You are returning from school, very tired or are just back from a long football session. Each muscle in your body longs for rest and you don't even feel like washing your face. In such situations, the television is a boon to us because it doesn't ask us any questions or expect anything from us. It just entertains us. With the remote control in hand, you are its master — just command, and it will respond!

At home, not only children but also the elderly sit glued to their seats while watching television and it almost becomes a habit. For many, it relaxes their mind and makes life more enjoyable.

Imagine you start watching television at the age 7 or 8, and continue till you are 80. Do you know how much time you would have spent on it? TEN Years!

On an average, each one of us spends almost ten years watching the television. If television is to take such a significant amount of our lifetime, we need to think twice – is watching television good or bad?

It's very difficult to answer this question because television, like many other technological innovations, is a mix of both good and bad!

Television is the window to the world—it brings the entire world to our drawing room. Be it global news, school and college lessons, sports, music, entertainment or edutainment—just ask for it and you will have it.

An effective tool of visual communication, the television can teach us several things—than what we gather from other sources of knowledge. Though this sounds good, you can't have too much of such goodness.

Television is believed to be a relaxant for the mind. But there is another side to it—researchers have found that once we start watching television, parts of our brain start sleeping within next few minutes. As a result, we absorb whatever is shown on the screen, without thinking over it.

All television and no creativity makes Jack a dull boy. We tend to lose interest in work and this may even cause depression. People tend to become couch potatoes, and binge on a lot of junk food. This leads to obesity, which forms a basis of several illnesses.

Television

Watching too much television also reduces valuable time we spend with our family and may lead to isolation of members within the family.

In fact, when we get into the habit of regular TV watching at a specified time every day, week after week, we become its slaves. This may sound very harsh but just try missing one of your favourite programmes for a day or two. See what kind of a stress it can put you to. Actually, when you miss a programme, you really don't miss out on anything; you can always watch it the next day, or the next week. But this is what TV addicts don't seem to understand.

Television is a friend that has found a place in our homes. But it is for us to decide whether we want it to use it as a friend or a foe.

Experts say we need to have some control on how much of television we watch every day. Even the little time we spend has to be of use to us. Mere channel surfing for the sake of killing time could become a bad habit, and may affect both our eyes and mind.

Just remember that there is a special button in the television's remote control, which we don't use very often – the 'switch off' button. Learn to use this button to your benefit – programme your TV viewing time!

Prodigy books

Biographies

Abdul Kalam
Charles Darwin
Marie Curie
Visvesvaraya
Srinivasa Ramanujan
Newton
Einstein
James Watt
Sir JC Bose
Alexander Graham Bell
Gandhi
Jawaharlal Nehru
Mother Teresa
Ambedkar
Bhagat Sigh
Tipu Sultan
Rani of Jhansi
Akbar
Shivaji
Bharati
Rabindranath Tagore
Martin Luther King
Alexander the Great
Napoleon
Adolf Hitler
Charlie Chaplin
Walt Disney
Bill Gates
Narayana Murthy
Columbus

Classics Retold

Homer's Iliad
The Odyssey
The Tempest
Hamlet
The Merchant of Venice
Twelfth Night
Romeo and Juliet
Macbeth

Other Titles

The Universe
Hinduism
Global Warming
Abraham Lincoln
The New 7 wonders of the World
Life
Tsunami
Dinosaurs
Ganga
World War II
Madras - Chennai
Exam Tips
Television
Effective Communication
Creative Thinking